American Dream or Mortgage Nightmare

American Dream or Mortgage Nightmare

◆

Techniques for buyers, sellers, agents and homeowners who want to avoid and recover from foreclosure!

Michelle Pettway

iUniverse, Inc.
New York Lincoln Shanghai

American Dream or Mortgage Nightmare
Techniques for buyers, sellers, agents and homeowners who want to avoid and recover from foreclosure!

iUniverse books may be ordered through booksellers or by contacting:

iUniverse
2021 Pine Lake Road, Suite 100
Lincoln, NE 68512
www.iuniverse.com
1-800-Authors (1-800-288-4677)

Because of the dynamic nature of the Internet, any Web addresses or links contained in this book may have changed since publication and may no longer be valid.

The information, ideas, and suggestions in this book are not intended to render professional advice. Before following any suggestions contained in this book, you should consult your personal accountant or other financial advisor. Neither the author nor the publisher shall be liable or responsible for any loss or damage allegedly arising as a consequence of your use or application of any information or suggestions in this book.

ISBN: 978-0-595-47954-2 (pbk)
ISBN: 978-0-595-60002-1 (ebk)

Printed in the United States of America

Contents

Acknowledgements

Thank God for strength, courage and wisdom!
Thank you to Saint Philip AME Church, Pastor George Moore
And Crown Financial Ministries

I'd like to thank my family, my husband Clift Pettway for supporting my dreams, my daughters Stephanie and Tiffany who worked side by side with me to complete this book.

None of this could have happened without the loving support and prayers from my mother.

I'd like to thank Michele Shoda, Lisa Lowell and my Solid Source Realty family who gave me the opportunity to advance my dreams and goals.

"Everything in the heavens and earth is yours O' Lord, and this is your kingdom. We adore you as being in control of everything. Riches and honor come from you alone, and you are the Ruler of all mankind; you hand controls power and might, and it is at your discretion that men are made great and given strength."
King David, I Chronicles 29:11–12

Introduction

When I received the call from my past clients informing me that they needed to sale the home that I had sold them just one year before, I had no idea how much trouble they were really in. I arrived at the home at nine that Monday morning. I entered the living room and to my surprise they had not purchased any furniture or decorated the home as many new homeowners do. I was greeted by the lady of the house and as customary for me during a listing appointment I asked her to walk me through their home. I wanted to see the condition of the house since I had not been there since we closed a year ago. As we entered into the bedrooms there were only mattresses on the floor and clothes in boxes. When I though it couldn't have gotten any worse we entered into the kitchen. While immaculate, there was something missing, the refrigerator. Where there was suppose to be a refrigerator laid a large cooler. As we walked through she pointed out that since they had purchased the home they had put every dollar of their income into the mortgage and other bills and had not been able to afford to purchase a refrigerator. She opened the cooler and inside there was a half dozen of eggs, a half gallon of milk, some sticks of butter and a few soft drinks on ice. My heart sank.

I knew at the closing something wasn't right. These particular clients had been referred to me by a friend. They had their mortgage broker in place when I meet them for the first time. It is usually my policy to refer a mortgage broker or lender that I already have a relationship with. I hadn't heard of this mortgage broker before but the clients seemed to be satisfied with him, so I also agreed to work with him.

We arrived at the attorney's office for closing at four in the afternoon, our scheduled time for the closing. When we arrived the loan documents had not been emailed to the closing attorney. I immediately pulled out my cell phone and dialed the broker to inquire about the delay. He told me that the underwriter was behind in processing but that everything would be complete in just a few minutes. We sat there for two additional hours before the closing began. Once the documents arrived and the attorney started the signing process, the buyers seemed extremely uncomfortable, not nervous or excited but uncomfortable. They seemed unfamiliar with the loan terms and payments. I asked that we stop the closing so that I could consult privately with my clients. We stepped into the lobby area where I asked them about their concerns. They stated that the monthly payment was considerably higher than they were told it would be. Again I pulled out my cell phone to contact the broker who had failed to attend the closing. He asked to speak with the buyers and he explained to them that the difference in the payment they that were quoted on their original good faith estimate and what they were given at the closing table was due to some unforeseen credit issues. They listened patiently and hung up. I couldn't go back in good conscious if I hadn't asked them if they wanted to walk away from this transaction. They did not. So we continued. We finally closed the transaction at nine that evening. The sellers were happy. The buyers seemed content and we all went our separate ways. Although I was very new in the business, I still felt something wasn't right. I year later I found out why.

As we sat on the carpeted floor of her living room she explained that she knew at the closing that they could not afford the house. They were excited about the opportunity to have a piece of the American dream. She told me how the loan officer had embellished their income to get them into the home, claiming slightly more overtime for her husband's job than he actually received. By the time they made it to the closing table they had fallen in love with the house and with the idea of homeownership. In their minds, they had made it one step closer to having the "American dream." Well the damage had been done and I felt as though it was now my job to help them fix it. We immediately put the home on the market and by the grace of GOD we secured a contract within thirty days. They were able to avoid foreclosure, move into an affordable apartment and began to live again.

"Any governments, like any family, can for a year spend a little more than it earns. But you and I know that a continuance of that habit means the poor-house."
Franklin D. Roosevelt 1932

Foreclosure

Before we can begin to understand foreclosure let us first define a "mort-gage." A mortgage essentially is composed of two parties. The "mortgagee" is the lender who holds the note on a piece of real estate. The "mortgagor" is the homeowner who obtains the loan for the piece of real estate. The "mortgage" is the loan agreement (written document of terms and condi-tions) that allows people to borrow the money to buy a home or other real estate. Loans are obtained through financial institutions such as a bank, a savings and loan company, an insurance company or most commonly a mortgage company.

"Foreclosure" is the process by in which a lender repossesses a piece of property. If a homeowner fails to pay for a number of months, the lender can begin the foreclosure process. In most cases the foreclosure process begins when the homeowner defaults for 90 days. Foreclosure laws vary from state to state. The process can take 30 to 365 days depending on the state in which the property is located. Some states may also have a redemp-tion period. A homeowner who may be in a foreclosure situation should research their state laws.

The foreclosure process can be both judicial and non judicial. The pro-cess usually begins with a NOD, a Notice of Default which is usually filed by the lender's attorney or trustee. A notice of default is filed at the record-ers court in the county in which the property is located. Following the NOD is a NOS. NOS is the Notice of Sale which is placed in a county publication, usually in the county in which the property is located. In the state of Georgia where I am located, ads for foreclosure sales are listed in each county news publication at least 30 days prior to the sale. Homes are then auctioned on the courthouse steps the first Tuesday of each month. If the property fails to sale at the courthouse auction, an attorney representing the lender will purchase the property on behalf of the lender and the property becomes a REO. REO is Real Estate Owned. The lender can then sale the property on the open market in an attempt to recuperate their funds. The foreclosure process can be quite costly for the lender. Foreclosure can cost lenders thousands of dollars.

For the homeowner this process in not only embarrassing but is also heartbreaking.

Elaine was the second call I had made that Tuesday morning. Her home had expired from the market the day before. After my brief introduction she explained that she desperately needed to sell her home before it foreclosed. After taking off much too much time from work to take care of her mother who was seriously ill, Elaine lost her job. She had missed three months of mortgage payments and the lender had begun the foreclosure process. Her previous real estate agent had listed the property at a fair market price but was unable to secure a contract. Because she did not have the funds available to commit to a work out plan with the lender, I explained to her that I thought a "short sale" would be a best course of action. I had Elaine contact her mortgage lender to ask if they would consider a "short sale" payoff. They would. Several days later I met with Elaine and we re-listed her home at a price just below market and I began aggressively marketing the property. Despite our efforts we had not gotten one showing in several weeks and it became apparent the home would be foreclosed on. I advised her that it was time for us to find another place to live for her and her family. Of course she was heart-broken, this had been her very first home and she had taken her time to decorate it and her plan was to someday leave it to her daughter. I let her know that this was a temporary setback but that she could still fulfill that dream. She would not be able to purchase a new home right away, but she was able to find a home to rent to start the rebuilding process. Later we will discuss options for homeowners who have gone through a foreclosure, how to pick up the pieces and rebuild their credit and make a fresh start. While it is not easy to do, sometimes a fresh start is all we need.

Foreclosure Trends

Unfortunately foreclosure is spreading through our communities like a plague. Just about everyone knows someone who has been affected by it in one way or another. Homeowners in communities around the country are facing a decrease in property value due to the enormous amount of foreclosures. Locally, the city of Atlanta zip code 30310 in my state of Georgia has one the highest foreclosure rates.

According to Marla Webb, at Foreclosure.com spokesperson, Georgia numbers are following a national trend, with foreclosure inventory nationwide up 10 percent compared to July 2004.

According to an article on realtytrac.com/pub/articles despite a 19 percent decrease in new foreclosures in March, Georgia documented the highest state foreclosure rate in the first quarter of 2006, this equates to one new foreclosure for every 127 households. James J. Saccacio, CEO of RealtyTrac says "The overall trend is toward escalating foreclosure rates, with 82 of the top 100 metro areas reporting year-over-year increases in the number of homes affected by foreclosure."

Top 10 states for foreclosure (August 2007) Via Realtytrac

1. Nevada 1 in 165 homes

2. California 1 in 224 homes

3. Florida 1 in 224 homes

4. Georgia 1 in 271 homes

5. Ohio 1 in 281 homes

6. Michigan 1 in 288 homes

7. Arizona 1 in 289 homes

8. Colorado 1 in 312 homes

9. Texas 1 in 532 homes

10. Indiana 1 in 544 homes

Reasons for Foreclosure

Before we can begin to discuss foreclosure prevention, we must first explore the reasons for the number of increasing foreclosures. The four most common reasons for foreclosure are illness, death, job loss and divorce. While we certainly can not predict illness, death and in most cases Job loss, however, in some cases divorce happens long before someone finally says "I want a divorce."

My friend and her husband had been having problems for several years. I think like a lot of couples, they thought it would be better to stay together "for the kids." By the time they realized it would not be in anyone's best interest to stay together the situation had become extremely hostile. In a hostile divorce situation it is almost impossible to agree on anything, and not only did the children suffer but out the window went the finances and credit for both of them. Even though my friend's husband left her the house, he left her with a home that she could not afford; after all, they were a household that functioned with a two person income. On more than one occasion I have heard people say "when purchasing a home, you should obtain a mortgage payment that could be paid with one person's income even if you are in two income family." I thought at the time that was a little presumptuous, but I don't anymore. I know say "prepare for the worst and always pray for the best." Unfortunately she lost the home to foreclosure, but they have both individually gotten a new start and are both finding their own way.

It is important to remember that if you are facing any of these situations your creditors need to know. As soon as a homeowner knows that there is going to be a problem, they should contact their mortgage lender. Often lenders are willing to work with homeowners, the earlier a homeowner contacts the lender the better. The work-out options available to a homeowner decreases as the delinquency debt increases.

PREDATORY LENDERS

Predatory lenders are those lenders who use deception to convince homebuyers to enter into loan programs that are unfair and designed to be beneficial to the lender but detrimental to the borrower. Predatory lenders not only work through home loans, but payday loans, car title loans and credit cards. Such lenders usually target people with little, bad or no credit, low income, limited education or limited knowledge of the industry. Targets of these acts of injustice. In the case of car title loans and mortgages, the terms are designed to make it almost impossible to fulfill a payoff. The lenders then foreclosures or repossess the property used for collateral for the loans. Most of these types of loans come with enormous and sometimes ridiculous interest rates. I have fallen not once, not twice but three times for a predatory lending. The first time, we were new to the Atlanta area. My husband and I had just gotten our first apartment and we needed furniture and electronics. At that time VCRs were all the rage, but we had very little money and no credit. Someone introduced us to the world of rent-to-own. The next Saturday morning we went down to the local rent to own store and entered into an agreement to rent to own a VCR. Big mistake, without a full understanding of the enormous interest rate we ended up paying nearly a thousand dollars for a VCR with a purchase price of one hundred and fifty dollars. The second time, we borrowed two hundred dollars from a local "loan place" whereby it took us nearly a year of making payments to pay it off. THE THIRD TIME, we were strapped for cash and decided to get a car title loan on the car we had purchased cash just a year before. We were given a nine hundred dollar loan in which we paid on for nearly two years (without making a real dent in the balance, due to the enormous interest rate) and finally after missing two payments the car was repossessed. Lesson learned, stay away from predatory lenders.

In the next section we will discuss the impact interest rates can have on loan repayment and foreclosures.

ADJUSTABLE RATE MORTGAGES

In the last few years the number of foreclosures has increased in part because of what is known as ARM, Adjustable Rate Mortgage. An ARM is mortgage loan that has an interest rate that raises or lowers the note periodically according to the index. The index is commonly determined by one of the following;

- MTA–Monthly Treasure Average (based on 12 months)
- CODI–Cost of Deposit Index
- COFI–The 11th District Cost of Funds Index
- COSI–Cost of Savings Index

Applying an index on a rate plus margin basis means that the interest rate will equal the underlying index plus a margin. The margin will remain fixed for the life of the loan but the index will fluctuate. Margins are locked in when your loan closes. One such example is the LIBOR. LIBOR refers to London Interbank Offered Rate. On a LIBOR of LIBOR plus 3%, 3% would be the fixed rate and LIBOR would adjust. In this case the LIBOR is the index. The problem with this loan is that the payments would adjust monthly and homeowners could not predict the payment from month to month.

More common ARMs come with a fixed rate for two to five years, here is the problem. Homeowners were offered lower rates in the beginning of the loan. That is great because homeowners were able to purchase homes at a price that may have otherwise been unaffordable. For example, a purchaser qualifies for a home with a purchase price of $150,000 and is based on an interested rate of 7% they would have a payment of $998.00 principal and interest, the same purchaser could purchase a home for $186,000 with a rate of 5% and have the same payment. In the case of an ARM that will adjust in say two years by 2%, if the purchaser opted to buy the home with a purchase price of $186,000, after two years their payment would increase to $1238.00. This is a significant difference in the budget of many American homes. I saw this in the case of my good friend Asha. Asha had actually purchased a home with a great 7% fixed interest rate, however when interest rates dropped to an "all time low" she decided to refinance into a 5 percent ARM. She did not read the fine print and today she is at 9% and climbing with no opportunity to refinance because of late payments, lack of equity and foreclosures in her immediate area.

ARMs are a fantastic tool if they are handled properly. Many homeowners entered into these types of loans under the pretence that they could refinance before the interest rate adjust. The problem is many homeowners were not properly aware of the criteria needed to refinance. First, homeowners must maintain a good credit rating in order to refinance into a better loan. Secondly, homeowners need to have money saved in that some refinance loans may come with expenses such as application fees, appraisal fees and closing cost. And lastly, the property must maintain or in some cases increase in value, something homeowners may not have any control over.

Tips to homebuyers

- *Whenever possible, lock into a 15 or 30 year fixed interest rate*
- *If choosing an adjustable rate make sure you are aware of when your interest will adjust, how much it will adjust and what the "cap" rate will be.*

- *When looking to refinance before the rate adjust be sure to maintain good credit, save money and keep the home in great condition.*

- *Make sure that your income is enough to cover your payment if and when the interest rate adjusts.*

SUBPRIME LENDING

To fully understand why one would enter into an Adjustable Rate Mortgage that may not be in their best interest, we must explore Subprime Lending. Subprime lending also known as "second chance lending" or "B-paper" is a practice whereby lenders offer loans to borrowers who can not qualify under traditional terms. These borrowers typically have slow or bad credit and may be self employed. Due the high interest rates and slow or bad credit of the borrower, subprime lending is risky for the lender and the borrower. For all parties there is an increased chance of default and foreclosure. While slightly similar to predatory lending, subprime lending is a lot less aggressive.

As part of the Subprime loans borrowers were offered a low interest rate in the beginning of the loan and it would adjust to a higher interest rate in a certain number of months or years. Ultimately this practice has led to an awful increase in the number of foreclosures and has forced many subprime lenders and a few primary lenders to close their doors. In 2006 Homebanc (not a traditional subprime lender) one of the Southeast Region's largest lenders closed their doors along with hundreds of other lenders who experienced massive layoffs, completely shut down or sought bankruptcy protection.

Tips of homebuyers

- *If possible use primary or "A paper" lenders*

- *Contact Experian, Transunion and Equifax for a credit report early and often*

- *Dispute items on your credit report that are not correct*

- *Begin improving your credit a least two year prior to applying for a home loan*

- *Avoid changing jobs or careers when looking to purchase a home*

- *If self-employed, keep proper business documentation and file taxes every year*

The other culprit

The other culprit that has wreaked havoc on our economy and has cost lenders and homeowners millions of dollars is mortgage fraud. In the next section we will spend quite a bit of time exploring mortgage fraud and its impact on our economy and the lending industry.

MORTGAGE FRAUD

"Wealth obtained by fraud dwindles"
Proverbs 13:11

IF YOU THINK YOU ARE THE VICTIM OF MORTGAGE FRAUD CONTACT THE ATTORNEY GENERAL'S OFFICE

Mortgage fraud can be as subtle as a little white lie on the loan application or as involved as "straw buyers" and "straw sellers." In this chapter we will explore many forms of mortgage fraud and how agents, buyers and sellers can protect themselves.

As I listened to a young man on the 6 o'clock news, he explained how he had formerly been a loan officer and how embarrassed he was at the things that he had participated in while working with a mortgage broker. He explained how he was encouraged to "manipulate the numbers," by reporting more income than a borrower actually had. How is this possible? No Doc Loans, Low Doc and Stated Income Loans, while these types of loans usually require a good credit score they also require very little or no written proof of income. For example, a homeowner may go in for a home loan and have a 750 credit, which is good by most standards, but may only have income of $22,000 per year. With that amount income a borrower may be limited to a condo, townhome or a fixer upper depending on the market. According to the young man on the news, in such a situation he was advised, even encouraged to document more income or overtime on a loan application to allow the borrower to qualify for more house. This is mortgage fraud. Any kind of misrepresentation on a loan application can be construed as mortgage fraud, especially if the false information provided helps a homeowner obtain a loan. This kind of mortgage fraud can lead directly to foreclosure as the homeowner may not be financially able to repay the loan.

Tips of homeowners

- *Report your income accurately*

- *Use reputable lenders, referrals are a great way to find reputable professionals*

- *Start small and build up (the average homeowner keeps their first home for 5 to 7 years and than upgrades to a larger home.)*

"Straw Buyers" —Property flipping SCAMS

"Flipping property" is technically not illegal by any means. As a matter of fact it is how many investors operate their real estate business. Flipping is similar to buying and selling stock, the concept is one in the same, buy low and sell higher. The most legitimate flippers purchase a piece of property at a low price, renovate and resale for a slightly higher price, a fair market price. That act in itself is okay. In the case of illegal flipping, there are many players, usually the appraiser, the loan officer (broker) and in some cases the real estate agent are all participants in the scam. Either a lender or real estate agent will solicit buyers who have fair to good credit; they offer them the opportunity to become an investor or homeowner. These buyers are known as "straw buyers." Scammers would target people who were homeless, mentally unstable or who had very little education. They would promise the "straw buyer" some amount of money at the closing and the promise of owning properties. A property is located, and the "straw buyer" makes an offer higher than the asking price. For example; the list price may be $100,000 the "straw buyer is encouraged to make an offer of $150,000 sighting that they will use the difference of $50,000 for repairs and upgrades. In comes the appraiser (usually in on the scam) to appraise the property. The planted appraiser knows going in that the home's value is only worth $100,000, but in order for the scam to work he must give it an appraised value of $150,000. The appraiser is also promised a monetary payoff for his efforts. At the closing the unsuspecting seller the home to the "straw buyer" for $150,000. The homeowners pays off his mortgage, takes whatever profit is due to him/her from the $100,000 and the $50,000 difference is paid to the "straw buyer." The "straw buyer is usually accompanied to the bank by the loan officer or real estate agent to cash the check, the "straw buyer is given a couple thousand dollars and the remainder is split between all other parties in the scam. In most cases the "straw buyer" never moves into the property and in some cases has never seen the property. If it is suppose to be an investment property, the "straw buyer" is told that they will be assisted in finding a renter for their investment property, but that never materializes and the property eventually goes into foreclosure. Homeowners and real estate agent beware, if seems too good to be true ... If someone offers to purchase a property far above asking price, there is a problem, even if they want to upgrade or make repairs. In that case, the buyer should purchase the property at asking price and refinance or get an equity line of credit after the initial closing. Remember it is also fraudulent for a seller to give a buyer a repair or upgrade allowance if the buyer does not use the allotted money for that purpose.

"But those who want to get rich fall into temptation and a snare and many foolish and harmful desires which plunge men into ruin." I Timothy 6:9

"Straw Sellers"

While there have not been as many cases of the "straw seller" scam, it is out there. Here is how it works. A "straw seller" usually targets a home that is a vacant or a family's summer home, he/she will research the county tax records to obtain owner information. The "straw seller" will gain entry into the home in some cases begin living there, he/she will obtain ID in the name of the owner and list the home with a real estate agent, who is in some cases in on the scam. They will list the home at a price above what is owed on the mortgage. The rest is easy. The "straw seller" with his fake ID sells the home to an unsuspecting buyer. The "straw seller" walks away with the profit from the sell and disappears. You can image what happens when the rightful owner returns to their home only to find another family living there, not to mention the mortgage nightmare that has been created. It may take the mortgage companies' years to correct the amount of damage that has been done.

Prevention is key! Tips for absentee homeowners.

- *Never leave personal documents in an unoccupied vacation or summer home*
- *Keep an active alarm system in your home*
- *Have a neighbor watch your home and notify you of any suspicious activity*
- *Find a reputable house sitter or service to visit the home periodically*
- *Secure locks and windows before you leave*
- *Use automated lighting systems*

Alternatives to foreclosure

✦

Eight alternatives to foreclosure.

REFINANCE

The first is to refinance. Refinance means to replace the current home loan with a more favorable loan. If a homeowners knows that their payment will increase to due to a climbing interest rate, they may want to refinance before the adjustment. As discussed in an earlier chapter, it is a good idea to refinance into a fixed rate loan. Be sure to check with your current lender to see if there are any pre-payment penalties on your current loan. With a refinance the original loan will be paid off and new terms will be assigned. This is a great alternative to homeowners who have maintained good credit, saved money and who have equity in their home.

The first step is to locate a reputable refinance lender, ask friends and family for a referral. Next, gather your income, asset and liability information. The refinance lender will want the same documents required when purchasing a home, documents such as paystubs, tax returns, w'2s etc. I think it is a good idea to set an appointment to sit down with your loan officer, avoid applying for a loan online if possible. After receiving your application and supporting documentation the loan officer will order an appraisal to determine the fair market value of your home. In some cases your home will need to appraise for more than the loan amount. The cost of the appraisal is usually paid by the borrower and cost between two and four hundred dollars. Just as with a purchase you will need to have homeowner's insurance and title insurance. Upon approval you will have a closing and you should be prepared to pay closing cost, this information should be provided to you by your loan officer early in the process. At the closing or shortly thereafter you will receive instructions for making your new payments.

RE-NEGOTIATION WITH CURRENT LENDER

While not as common, some lenders have been known to re-negotiate the terms of a loan with the homeowner. If your loan is in good standing but you know that your rate is about to increase you may want to contact your lender to re-negotiate. It doesn't hurt to ask. The lender may be willing to make an adjustment without the homeowner going through the entire refinance process. This process will help to save you money, because there is no appraisal fee or closing cost. you should be prepared to supply the lender with financial information to include income, liabilities, assets and banking information, if your loan is in good standing they may not require it. Remember this is not a refinance so if the lender agrees to adjust an interest rate or payment, get it in writing. Ask them to specify the new rate, new payment amount and length of time for the new rate. If possible you want the new rate to last for the duration of the loan.

FORBEARANCE AGREEMENT

Forbearance is a written repayment agreement between a lender and homeowner which contains a plan to reinstate a delinquent account. If you have fallen behind due to illness or unforeseen expenses but you believe you will be able to make future payment on time this might be a great option for you. Here is how it works. If your payments are normally $1000 a month and you have gotten behind two payments, for example purposes, you are behind on April and May's payments, and your lender agrees to a forbearance agreement, the lender will take your past due amount along with any late fees and divide it for a specify number of months. Usually a lender will give six months to year. Here is how it will look. Two missed payments plus late fees may total $2100 (for our example we will us 6 months) divided by 6 equals $350. For next 6 months beginning in June your payment will go from $1000 to $1350 allowing you to gradually make up the defaulted payments. In applying for a forbearance agreement you will be required to submit detailed financial information so that the lender is able to determine if the homeowner can qualify for a forbearance agreement. The lender wants to make sure that the new payment amount will not cause further hardship for you.

Advantages to a forbearance agreement

- *Homeowner is able to avoid foreclosure proceedings*

- *Homeowner is allowed to repay delinquent amount over time*

Disadvantages to a forbearance agreement

- *Homeowner's credit is negatively affected until delinquency is paid in full*

- *Homeowner monthly payment will increase for the agreed upon length of the repayment plan.*

PAYMENT DEFERMENT

While this option is more common with car loans, it is possible for some home loans. Check with your mortgage lender to see if this is an option. In this option the lender can defer one or more payments to the end of your loan. This is a great solution if you are having a temporary situation, like a layoff or illness. Some lenders will do this but allow you to pay the interest or a fee for that service, yet in still it is cheaper than some of your other options. Lenders who allow this option usually have a cap on it, meaning you can only apply for a deferment once a year or once every few years. Check with your lender for details.

DEED IN LIEU OF FORECLOSURE

Deed in lieu of foreclosure is a deed instrument in which the borrower conveys all interest in a property to the lender to satisfy a loan that is in default and avoid a foreclosure. A deed of lieu of foreclosure is a sort of voluntary repossession. Lenders will consider this option if the home can get fair market value. This option should not be entered to lightly and I think it is in the homeowner's best interest to explore all other options first. This instrument has to be in writing so if you are considering a deed in lieu of foreclosure contact a real estate attorney for assistance.

Advantage to the homeowner

- *The borrower avoids the public notoriety of a foreclosure proceeding*

Disadvantage to the homeowner

- *Negative credit reporting, this looks similar to a foreclosure of your credit*

Advantages to the lender

- *Because foreclosure can be costly to a lender, the lender may save money with this procedure.*

Disadvantage to the lender

- *The lender now has a REO property to sell, lender are in business of loans not selling property*

SELL YOUR HOME

It may be a good idea for a homeowner who foresees a problem with mortgage payments to consider selling their home. If you can sell your home before the loan goes into default, you may be able to purchase a more affordable home right away. Any homeowner who is considering selling a home should seek the assistance of a reputable and professional real estate agent. Many homeowners neglect to hire a real estate agent because they do not have or do not want to pay a real estate commission. I believe it is a small price to pay for the peace of mine a professional real estate can bring. Real estate agents usually have a list of reputable vendors who help to make it a smooth transaction. Ask your real estate agent if they have a list of lenders, appraisers, home inspectors and pest control agents who can assist in the process. Listing agents are also aware of the state laws, market conditions and can provide necessary documents to execute the transaction.

Tips for selling your home

- *Enlist the help of a professional real estate agent*
- *Price the home competitively from the start of the listing. An appraisal my be helpful in determining a list price*
- *De-clutter and clean each room—consider hiring a professional stager*
- *De-personalize the home, by removing pictures and other personal items*
- *Make sure your real estate agent can advertise your home on major real estate websites*
- *Make sure your agent has a good marketing plan that will span the length of the listing.*
- *Cooperate with agents who want to show prospective buyers your home*
- *Keep pets outside, your leave them with a friend during the listing period*
- *Keep your home in clean, neat and in show condition everyday, first impressions are everything when homebuyers are looking at your home*

SHORT SALE

Short sales are becoming increasingly popular in our society; therefore we will spend some time exploring the short sale option. A short sale is when a lender holding the mortgage on a piece of property agrees to settle for a lesser amount as a payoff because the outstanding debt on a property is greater than the market value of the property. Often times a lender is willing to negotiate a short sale when the property is in pre-foreclosure status or when the property value has been lowered due to several foreclosures in that immediate area.

Seller Advantages for a short sale

- *By lowering the price of the seller's home, it becomes more attractive to buyers*
- *Seller is able for avoid foreclosure*
- *Seller reduces the amount of debt owed on the property*
- *Seller will suffer less damage to their credit score*

The IRS may consider debt forgiveness as income. The seller will have to pay taxes on this amount that is forgiven and there is no guarantee that a lender who accepts a short sale will not legally pursue a borrower for the difference between the amount owed and the amount paid. For example, if a seller owes $100,000 on a piece of property in which the lender agrees to settle for $80,000 the seller is now responsible to pay taxes on the $20,000 difference and or may be forced to pay the $20,000 difference to the lender.

Please visit <u>www.irs.gov</u> for more information and tax laws

If a homeowner is seeking a short sale option they should enlist the help of a professional real agent or consultant with short sale experience for assistance. This process is usually far more complicated than the average sell. Just as a forbearance agreement requires that a seller submit personal and financial information, the same holds true for a short sale. In most cases a homeowner requesting a short sale is doing so because they can no longer afford the home. The lender will require that the homeowners complete a "Short Sale Packet." A short package is a set of documents that the lender will send to the seller to request a short sale payoff. The seller will be asked to provide the following information;

1. Income

2. Assets

3. Liabilities

4. Proof of employment or lack there of

5. Bank statements

6. Hardship letter–a letter explaining the reasons for financial distress.

After receiving the required documents along with an offer from a potential buyer the lender will request a BPO–Broker Price Opinion to determine a fair selling price for the home. This is not as detailed as an appraisal but it insures the lender that the offer being made is reasonable. When the listing agent presents the offer to the lender, it most also be accompanied by a HUD-1 settlement state. This lets the lender know their bottom line figure. All expenses should be included. Let me tell you what happened to a real estate colleague of mine who was involved in a short sale transaction.

Jennifer and her client had received permission from her client's lender to sell the property for a short sale value. Several weeks after listing the home they received an offer. After the closing attorney prepared a HUD-1 which included the necessary expenses to sell the property, Jennifer submitted all the necessary information to the homeowner's lender. The HUD-1 stated that the lender would receive a net payoff of approximately $86,700, considering the homeowner only owed $91,000 the bank accepted the offer and sent the closing attorney a payoff acceptance letter and wiring instructions. About one week before the closing the buyer had a termite inspection done, and the home was found to have termites and termite damage with a cost to cure of a little over $2000. The sellers (homeowners) who were in pre-foreclosure did not have the money for this expense, the buyers refused to pay as it was not part of the original agreement, the lender who had already agreed to a short sale payoff also refused to pay it. As you have probably guessed the real estate agent (my colleague) had to eat the cost of treatment and repair from her real estate commission. Lesson well learned.

It is crucial that you enlist the help of a real estate preferably one with short sale experience if you considering this as an option. Be sure to have your home inspected for necessary and unforeseen expenses prior to submitting a payoff quote to the lender. Prior to listing decide if you are willing and able to make repairs or if you want to sell the property "as is." Remember lenders are not in the repair business, and they usually want a clean offer free of contingencies and stipulations. These are all items that an agent experienced with short sales can discuss with you.

BANKRUPTCY

Homeowners who are having difficulty making mortgage payments may also have trouble with other household expenses. For some the answer may be a fresh start. If someone is seeking bankruptcy as an option to recover from debt and avoid foreclosure or repossession, they should consult an Attorney. Bankruptcy is a legally declared inability of an individual or organizations to pay their debtors. Creditors may file a bankruptcy petition against a debtor in an effort to recuperate some portion of what they are owed. In most cases, however, bankruptcy is initiated by the debtor. A Homeowner may be able to avoid foreclosure when filing bankruptcy (depending on the type of bankruptcy filed.) There are generally two types of bankruptcy cases an individual can file, Chapter 7 or Chapter 13. Please seek professional legal advice from a bankruptcy attorney. In the next section will discuss Chapter 7 versus Chapter 13. Bankruptcy should be a final option as most bankruptcy filings will remain on your credit report for ten years. Sometimes however, if you are consumed with debt, this is the best option. You can also seek the help of a financial advisor or debt consolidator. Debt consolidators may be able to get decreases in interest rates and payments without filing a bankruptcy.

Chapter 7

This chapter of a Bankruptcy calls for liquidation of assets, this is, the sale of a debtor's nonexempt properties (a home, boat, car etc) and the distribution of the proceeds of the sale to creditors. Chapter 7 starts with the debtor filing a petition with the bankruptcy court serving the area where the individual resides. The debtor must also file with the court schedules of assets and liabilities, a schedule of income and expenses, a statement of financial affairs; and a schedule of contracts and unexpired leases as in the case of rental or investment properties. Debtors must also provide tax return information for the current year as well as previous years. They must file: a certificate of credit counseling from a reputable credit counseling service. A complete list of filing documents can be provided by your Attorney or by visiting www.uscourts.gov/bankruptcy.com

Chapter 13

Chapter 13 bankruptcy is for the most part a plan to repay your debt. A person can file a Chapter 13 bankruptcy in Federal Court. Certain properties are exempt from repossession. After the initial filing the Chapter 13 bankruptcy, the Court can issue an Automatic Stay, this Stay will require that all collection proceedings cease. Debtors may be allowed to remain in their homes and repay the delinquency on their mortgage payment, debtors are required to repay past due mortgage payments as well as continue to make future mortgage payments. There are exceptions to the Automatic Stay in the case where a debtor files multiple bankruptcies back to back. In the event this happens they debtor may only have Stay protection for only thirty days. It is essential to provide all necessary documentation upon first filing and avoid filing multiple bankruptcy cases.

FHA LOANS
FHA—FEDERAL HOUSING ADMINISTRATION

FHA does not make loans but they insure loans for borrowers who qualify. Homeowners who have loans secured by FHA have an advantage. A portion of their monthly mortgage payment goes to a program that is designed to help homeowners who are in a foreclosure situation. If a homeowner has a FHA secured loan and foresees a problem with making mortgage payments that can contact their lender for assistance or they can speak with a FHA counselor. Many FHA counselors are free of charge, if there is a fee it is nominal. These counselors can assist with:

- *Review your financial situation and determine what options are available to you.*

- *Learn which of the various workout arrangements lenders consider makes the most sense for you and your family.*

- *Contact the lender with you or on your behalf to discuss a workout plan*

- *Protect you from future credit problems before you get too far behind on mortgage payments*

Just as with other types of loans a homeowner may be able to enter into a forbearance agreement to reinstate their account. A forbearance agreement to reinstate a delinquent account is most effective if the problem is short term such as a brief illness or short term layoff. If the problems is long term it may be a good idea to have the FHA counsel negotiate one the following options:

- *Mortgage modification*

- *Partial Claim*

Mortgage modification, if a homeowner can make payments on the loan, but can't afford to bring the account current or they can't afford the current payment, the lender may be able be permanently change the loan in one or more of the following ways:

- *Adding the missed payments to the existing loan balance.*
- *Changing the interest rate, including making an adjustable rate into a fixed rate.*
- *Extending the number of years you have to repay*

Partial claim, if the mortgage is insured, a lender may be able help a homeowner get a one-time interest-free loan from the mortgage guarantor to bring the account current. They may be allowed to wait several years before repaying this loan. A homeowner can qualify for an FHA partial claim if:

- *The loan is between 4 and 12 months delinquent*
- *The homeowner is able to begin making full mortgage payments again*

If a homeowner's lender files a partial claim, HUD will pay the lender the amount of money necessary to bring the mortgage current. The homeowner must sign a promissory note, and a lien will be placed on your property until the promissory note is paid in full. The promissory note is interest-free. For more information, go to www.fha.gov/foreclosure.

FHA is also offering refinancing options for homeowners with good credit you can not afford their mortgage payments.

THE PRESIDENT'S PLAN

The Bush administration released a foreclosure relief plan that could help 1.2 million distressed homeowners.

President George Bush and Treasury Secretary Henry Paulson said the plan will streamline the mortgage modification process for many distressed homeowners. The plan should bring more relief to more homeowners in a timely manner. The plan will include a five-year freeze on interest rates for homeowners who are current on their monthly payments. The freeze is limited however. The plan excludes anyone more than 30 days late at the time the mortgage would be modified or anyone who has been more than 60 days late at any time within the previous 12 months.

The plan only covers homeowners with adjustable rate mortgages resetting beginning in 2008 and eliminates anyone who is judged capable of continuing to make mortgage payments at the higher reset rates.

It is estimated that of the 2 million subprime ARMS that are expected to reset through the end of 2009, only 240,000 of those would be covered by the freeze.

Recovering from foreclosure

Sometimes foreclosure unfortunately is unavoidable. There is life after foreclosure. Start immediately to rebuild your credit. It is a good idea to locate a new home or an apartment before the foreclosure has been updated on the credit report. Depending on your credit, finding a new home may present some challenges, apartment communities can be difficult to get into because of the mortgage payment history. In that case finding a private investor with rental property is a great option. There are investors who will also allow for a "Lease Purchase" option. This option with allow a person to enter into a contract whereby that can make an upfront down payment (optional) on a piece of property in which they agree to purchase after a certain amount of time. If you choose a lease purchase it is a good idea to ask for at least two years. Two years of on-time payments will go along way to help rebuild your credit. Consult a real estate with knowledge of the "lease purchase" option for assistance. Don't give up even though foreclosure can be depressing and in some cases traumatic for the family. Don't give up on your dream. Don't give up on what has been promised to all us who have faith and believe that we were not put here to struggle and live in poverty.

We have had the opportunity to discuss the reasons for foreclosure and explore options to avoid foreclosure. In the chapter we will discuss ending the cycle. What we can do to secure our future, not just to live the "American Dream" that we have for ourselves but the dream that the Lord as has always had for his children. I did not want to bombard my readers with quotes and scriptures from the bible, but I do want you to know that I feel we survive through Christ. I believe to begin to pick up the pieces of any tragedy we must begin with prayer first. I learned years ago that the answer in not to pray to stop foreclosure or to pray for more money, but to pray for wisdom, guidance, physical strength, emotional strength, love, peace, blessing and favor from the Lord. With these things all things are possible. I learned in my Crown Financial Ministries Class that all that I own, I do not own, but it is the Lord's and he has loaned it to me for a time. If I am a good Sheppard and I am great with small things he will bless me with more. I want to pass these things to you know matter what your situation is. I don't want to preach or lecture, I just want to let you know how I survive. I have utilized some of the options that I discuss in this book, but I started first by praying for wisdom and guidance. We will discuss this more and the end of this chapter.

End the Cycle

Begin the home buying process two years in advance

I have had the great fortune of working with many first time homebuyers. It is one of the reasons I remain in real estate. There is no greater feeling for me than seeing the look on a homebuyers face when you walk them into the home of their dreams. They know from the front door that this is the home they want to live in, raise their children in, where they want to host endless holiday parties and cook-outs and rest in at the end of a long day. For many first time buyers this process begins with an internet search just days or weeks before they are ready to start the search for a new home. When looking to purchase your first home, start early. Give yourself two years to build the highest credit score possible. Check your credit report early and as often as every six month to watch for errors. Learn the things that will negatively impact your credit. See below 5 ways to increase and maintain a great credit score.

- *Make timely payments on all credit accounts, mail-in payments should be post dated at least 10 days prior to payment due date.*
- *Have at least three lines of credit*
- *Credit balance should be at least 25%-30% of your credit limit, for example if you have a credit card with a maximum limit of $900 your balance should not exceed $300*
- *Don't kill your debt ratio by opening too many accounts or co-signing for others*

- *Avoid paying off Credit Cards at one time, creditors like to see that you can make scheduled payments.*

Have at least two years of employment on the same job or in the same field. Mortgage lenders like to see job/career stability. These things will insure the opportunity to get better financing with the best interest rates.

File your taxes yearly and keep accurate accounting records if you are self-employed!

Filing your taxes and paying your tax debt is essential to the home buying process. Mortgage lenders do not want to see tax liens and judgments on your credit report. Equally as important you must have an accurate accounting of your business finances. It may be a good idea to seek the assistance of a financial advisor or accountant.

Open a saving account strictly for the purpose of purchasing a home

"NO DOWN PAYMENT" does not mean buy a house with NO MONEY. There are several items a homebuyer should be prepared to pay for. More often than not, lenders will require an application fee and an appraisal fee. These fees alone can cost a buyer over four hundred dollars. A professional real estate agent will always suggest that the buyer obtain a home inspection, termite inspection and in some cases a survey. These expenses can easily exceed a thousand dollars. Although in some states earnest money is not required, many sellers are more likely to accept an offer that is sealed with an earnest money contribution from the buyer. Earnest money can be as little as a couple of hundred dollars to 10 to 25 percent of the purchase price.

Many down payment assistance programs are being eliminated and first time buyers have to bring their down payment to the transaction. A down payment can be as little a 3% of the purchase to as much as 20% depending on loan type and credit history. It is also a good idea to understand the different types of loans. With good credit and money saved, the world is your oyster.

Seek wise counsel–hire reputable agents and lenders to represent you!

"Listen to advice and accept instruction, and in the end you will be wise" Proverbs 19:20

It is an excellent idea to ask friends and family members who have recently purchased a home for a referral of a good loan officer and real estate agent. If you are not in a position to do so, be sure to interview at least three agents, ask for references. If you are working with an agent who is new to the business ask for character references from previous co-workers, friends and family. You should use the same care to hire a loan officer and real estate agent as you use to hire a your family doctor or legal attorney. Agents should also have a resume or list of references prepared as a part of their buyer and seller presentation. Your agent should also supply you with the names of numbers of reputable home inspectors, surveyors, handymen and other vendors required to complete the transaction. As well your loan officer should be able to provide you an appraiser who can determine the fair market value of the home in which you wish to purchase. Avoid finding a loan officer and real estate agent online. It is great to search and view homes online to save time and possibly money, with the enormous gas prices, but when it comes time to act you should sit down face to face with your loan officer and real estate agent. Also the number of scams executed against consumers online has increased drastically over the past few years, it is not a good idea to give to much personal information over the internet, especially if you are unsure of who is on the receiving end. Your real estate agent will usually have a real estate website in which you can safely and securely search for homes. Some of these sites will have mortgage calculators and other links to help you with home buying or selling process.

Having a giving heart

"There is one who scatters, yet increases all the more, and there is one who withholds what is justly due, but it results only in want. The generous man will be prosperous, and he who waters will himself be watered" Proverbs 11: 24–25

I could not get through this book without testifying to the greatness that my faith has brought to me. I can write about these situations because at some point in our lives we have lived it. My husband and I have been the homeowners on the verge of foreclosure. We have been the homebuyers who did not seek wise counsel, even the homeowners who had to file bankruptcy. It is only by the grace of my God that we have survived it all. We believe that we only survived the storms because we have faith and a giving heart. We believe that if we bless the Lord and his people we will be blessed, and we have been and continue to be blessed. Be faithful with few things (your credit, savings, giving and wise counsel) and The Lord will bless you with greatness.

"His Lord said unto him, well done, thou good and faithful servant: thou hast been faithful over a few things, I will make thee ruler many things: enter thou into the joy of thy Lord" Matthew 25:21

Spread the knowledge. Share this information with your children and children of the world. It is unfortunate that many of us do not learn to manage money, learn to save, learn to invest, learn give, learn to tithe when we are in our formative years, even our adolescent years and for some not even by our teenage years. But instead only in the years after we have made costly mistakes do we learn these valuable techniques.

"Train up a child in the way he should go: and when he is old, he will not depart from it" Proverbs 22:6 Remember the Lord has a dream for you, one that fair surpasses "The America Dream" A dream of great wealth, not poverty.

Resources

1. Howard Dayton *Your Money Counts* (Tyndale House Publishing, 1979) p.33

2. King James Version *The Holy Bible* (Elm Hill Press 1977)

3. The World Book Encyclopedia (World Book 2005) p.820

4. www.foreclosure.com

5. www.realtytrac.com

6. www.wikepedia.com

7. www.uscourts.gov/bankruptcycourts/bankruptcybasics/chapter7

8. www.therealestatebloggers.com

9. www.bankersonline.com

10. www.money.cnn.com

978-0-595-47954-2
0-595-47954-5

www.ingramcontent.com/pod-product-compliance
Lightning Source LLC
Chambersburg PA
CBHW021046180526
45163CB00005B/2301